LAGRANGE COUNTY PUBLIC LIBRARY
LGR j641.8 LAN 150093
Landau   Pizza :   the pie that's not a

3 0477 0001 8012 9

OFFICIAL DISCARD
LaGrange County Public Library

Y0-CUP-552

Pizza

The Pie that's not a Dessert

Elaine Landau

THE ROURKE PRESS, INC.
VERO BEACH, FLORIDA 32964

© 2001 The Rourke Press, Inc

All rights reserved. No part of this book may be reproduced or utilized in any form or by any means, electronic or mechanical including photocopying, recording or by any infomation storage and retrieval system without permission in writing from the publisher

PHOTO CREDITS
Ben Klaffke

EDITORIAL SERVICES
Editorial Directions Inc.

Library of Congress Cataloging-in-Publication Data

Landau, Elaine.
   Pizza : the pie that's not a desert / Elaine Landau.
     p. cm. — (Tasty treats)
   Includes bibliographical references.
   Summary: An introduction to the popular food, pizza, describing its history, variations, and "fun facts."
   ISBN 1-57103-339-4
   1. Pizza—Juvenile literature. [1. Pizza.] I. Title.

TX770.P58 L36 2000
641.8'24—dc21
                                                 00–022391

Printed in the USA

Contents

Kids and Pizza 5

Pizza History 7

Tasty and Healthy 11

Pizza Toppings 16

Pizza Fun Facts 20

Glossary 22

For Further Reading 23

Index 24

Would you like to sink your teeth into this slice of pizza?

Kids and Pizza

Do you like pizza? Many young people do. Pizza is not just served in pizza parlors. It is also a favorite in school cafeterias.

Pizza is a popular school lunch choice.

Here people enjoy a weekend pizza picnic.

You see it in school-lunch rooms across America. Children choose it for lunch more often than any other food.

Pizza is also popular other places. It is often served at parties. Many people have pizza as a weekend treat. Half of all pizza is bought on Friday and Saturday.

One study showed that 82 percent of kids between ages three and eleven like pizza better than chicken nuggets. They also like it more than hot dogs, macaroni and cheese, and hamburgers.

Pizza History

Pizza is sometimes served in the White House. It is also eaten by royalty. But it did not start out that way. It began in Italy as a food for poor people.

The first pizzas were made with vegetables. These were baked on leftover bread. **Vendors** sold them to people who did not have ovens. Pizza was a handy food. You did not need an oven or even a knife and fork to eat it.

A tomato, cheese, and basil pizza.

An early pizza maker wanted to make a pie the colors of Italy's flag.

At first, there were no tomato and cheese pizzas. For many years, people incorrectly believed that tomatoes were poisonous. The first tomato and cheese pie was not made until 1889.

An Italian tavern-owner named Don Raffaele Esposito thought of it. He wanted to make a red, white, and green pizza. These are the colors of Italy's flag. So he used red tomatoes and white **mozzarella** cheese. He added green **basil** to complete the pie.

Here tomato sauce is placed on the dough

The Queen of Italy, Margherita Teresa Giovanni, loved the pizza. So Esposito named it after her. It became known as Margherita Pizza.

In time, pizza became popular with the upper classes. Marie Carolina was the wife of Ferdinand I of Sicily and Naples. She had pizza ovens built in the forest. The royal hunting parties preferred the wild ducks and **boars** that they killed. But Marie Carolina insisted on pizza!

It is hard to think of pizza and not think of Italy. But did it really come from there? Some now dispute that it did.

Today there is new research. It shows that the Vikings may have been eating pizza since the early 9th century AD. They enjoyed flat round crusts with a number of different toppings. The Vikings toasted their pizzas on stone platters placed in large pizza-style ovens.

Seafood pizza was thought to be a Viking favorite. But the toppings changed with the seasons. It all depended on what was available at the time.

It makes you stop and think. You may have eaten in pizza parlors many times. But can you picture a group of Vikings adventurers ordering a pizza?

Tasty and Healthy

Pizza tastes good. It is healthy, too. The cheese in pizza has protein. The crust's enriched flour has **carbohydrates** and vitamin B. There is also vitamin C in tomato sauce. Our bodies need these things. Pizza is a fun food – not a junk food.

You may want to eat this healthy food often.

The cheese in pizza is a good source of protein.

But you don't have to go out to buy a pizza. Or have it delivered to your home for that matter. You can make your own Quick & Easy Kid's Pizza. Just follow the directions below. Remember to ask an adult to help you use the oven.

Here is what you will need:

an English muffin (sliced)

some pizza sauce

4 black pitted olives

1/4 cup grated mozzarella cheese

Vegetables and cheese make pizza a healthy choice.

Here is what to do:

Preheat the oven to 350 F.

Place the English muffin on a cookie sheet.

Spoon enough pizza sauce over each half to cover it.

Cut the olives into small pieces. Place these on the sauce covering muffin halves.

Sprinkle the grated cheese over each muffin half.

Using a potholder, place in the oven for 3 minutes.

Remove and allow to cool a bit before eating.

You can have just one of these muffins or make a batch to enjoy with your friends.

A pizza maker throws dough into the air to make the pie's crust.

Pizza Toppings

There are many pizza toppings. Everyone has their favorites. But American kids like the following best:

1. Pepperoni
2. Extra cheese
3. Pork toppings
4. Mushrooms

People around the world also like pizza, but the toppings differ.

Pepperoni is a favorite topping.

The combination pizza has several toppings.

What you want on your pizza may depend on where you live. People in Thailand like seafood pizza.

They order it with shrimp, **squid,** or crab on top. Germans like sauerkraut, ham, and onions on their pizza. In Holland, ham, mushrooms, and tomato slices are a favorite topping. The French prefer cream, egg, and goat cheese pizza. Many Russians order their pizzas with **mackerel** and onions on them.

An Asian Delight pizza with sardines on it.

People in the U.S. really enjoy pizza.

Pizza **Fun Facts**

 Americans eat about 100 acres of pizza daily. They spend more than 24 billion on pizza each year.

Americans eat a lot of pepperoni pizza.

 The largest pizza on record was made by a company in South Africa. The pizza was 100 feet wide. That is almost the height of an eleven-story building.

 In India, elephants are used to deliver pizzas.

 In parts of Canada's Northwest Territories, snowmobiles deliver pizzas.

 You would need about 8,100 medium-sized pizzas to cover the area of a baseball diamond.

 Americans eat about 251,770,000 pounds of pepperoni each year. Much of that is on pizza.

Glossary

basil (BAZ el) – an herb often used on pizza

boars (borz) – a type of wild pigs

carbohydrates (kar boh HYE drates) – a group of foods that provide the body with energy

mackerel (MAK uh ruhl) – a type of fish found in the Atlantic Ocean

mozzarella (MOT zar EL la) – a soft, white, mild cheese

squid (skwid) – a ten-armed sea creature with a long slender body

vendors (VEN durz) – people who sell something

For Further Reading

D'Amico, Joan, and Karen Drummond. *The Science Chef: 100 Fun Recipes for Kids.* New York: Wiley & Sons, Inc., 1995.

Kalbacken, Joan. *The Food Pyramid.* Danbury, Connecticut: Children's Press, 1998.

Landau, Elaine. *Wheat.* Danbury, Connecticut: Children's Press, 1999.

Rotner, Shelley. *Hold the Anchovies! A Book about Pizza.* New York: Orchard Books, 1996.

Index

carbohydrates   11
cheese   6, 7, 8, 11, 13, 16, 18
flour   11
Italy   7, 8, 9
pepperoni   16, 20, 21
pizza parlors   5, 10
royalty   7
seafood pizza   10, 18
tomatoes   8, 11, 18
toppings   10, 16, 18